CLOSING THE GAP
BY BUILDING BRIDGES
FOR ORGANIZATIONAL AND
PERSONAL SUCCESS!

EARL MORRISON

outskirts
press

Closing The Gap by Building Bridges for Organizational and Personal Success!
All Rights Reserved.
Copyright © 2025 Earl Morrison
v2.0

The opinions expressed in this manuscript are solely the opinions of the author and do not represent the opinions or thoughts of the publisher. The author has represented and warranted full ownership and/or legal right to publish all the materials in this book.

This book may not be reproduced, transmitted, or stored in whole or in part by any means, including graphic, electronic, or mechanical without the express written consent of the publisher except in the case of brief quotations embodied in critical articles and reviews.

Outskirts Press, Inc.
http://www.outskirtspress.com

ISBN: 978-1-9772-6809-9

Cover Photo © 2025 www.gettyimages.com. All rights reserved - used with permission.

Outskirts Press and the "OP" logo are trademarks belonging to Outskirts Press, Inc.

PRINTED IN THE UNITED STATES OF AMERICA

Table of Contents

Introduction	i
Ego	1
Foundation	6
Character	14
Leadership	20
Generational	29
Communication	36
Mental Health	44
Accountability	54
Teamwork	61
Dealing with Difficult People	67
Connections	74
Consistency	81
Spiritual	89
Conclusion	94

Introduction

Over the last several years one of the biggest issues I have consistently heard is the gap between the old guard and the new/younger generations. Everyone has an opinion about the issue, but it never seems to be a productive solution to solving the problem. There is no doubt that there is a gap that has been continuously growing year after year and all we do is watch and criticize. The question at some point must be "What do we do about it"?

I firmly believe that to correct the issue we must understand a little bit about how we got here. To do that we are going to dissect several topics that many of us have allowed to create the gap in the first place. We are going to have to put aside all our biases and focus on the real need: to bring us closer by bridging the gap. This means we are going to take a hard look at our contributions as well as what we have allowed society to dictate in our quest to work, play, and live together.

One of the things I have learned throughout my lifetime is that we often create the very challenges that we are trying to overcome. This is because we develop our own habits, morals, and character and we often do not take into consideration what makes everyone else tick. Collectively we do not take the time to understand each other and learn where we learned and adapted our current behaviors and ideology from. We spend far too little time trying to understand each other as opposed to criticizing and bashing each other.

Please join me as we take some time to understand our gaps, why they exist, and how to close the gap! As you prepare to join me on this journey take a few minutes to set the right tone for your mindset. I would ask that you approach this with your ego in check, open-minded, and non-judgmental until the end. If we could learn to approach our challenges in this manner, I feel we could be on the right track to Bridge the Gap!

Ego

There is no doubt in my mind that over the years my ego has been a huge contributor in creating gaps in all aspects of my life. There have been times when I have allowed my ego to dictate how I interacted and treated people, and it was not good. Nor was it very conducive to building lasting relationships or partnerships. The problem was it took me a while to figure out what the common denominator was in those failed relationships/partnerships: yep, it was me. As leaders, we must constantly be on our toes, so we do not influence others in a negative or derogatory way.

It took me a while, but once I realized this, it made things easier as I learned to grow and develop my leadership and the influence that comes with that. I teach leadership classes and when I am teaching class, I ask them how many leaders I have in the room. Normally I will get half to most of the class that will respond that they are leaders. Keep in mind that my classes all focus on leadership or supervision in some way, shape, form, or fashion. What we forget is that everyone is a leader, of at least one, yourself. Even the ones who respond that they are leaders are not thinking in this capacity. This is why ego, and a healthy ego are so important in understanding how to close the gap in all factions. People are reluctant to even say they are leaders for fear of negative reprisal or stereotype of arrogance or conceit. This is from our own collective issues and then we pair that with like-minded people who would rather blame everything and everyone for our lack of connection. We end up creating bigger and wider gaps than bridging or closing them. Part of the issue is we need to learn to get out of our own way. We will discuss ways that can be done a little later in the book.

How do we create and maintain a healthy ego that does not rear its ugly head? We must accept that each of us is different, and we come from all walks of life. We have all had similar and different influences that have shaped our beliefs and character. At some point, we establish who we are as individuals and determine what is acceptable for each of us. Far too often we allow others or society to dictate some of these things to us. So, the first thing is we must understand that we are all different and have our own ideas, thoughts, beliefs, and biases. What makes us work is the very fact that we are different and bring all our differences collectively to get the best of the best. Unfortunately, we often forget this and allow the negative bias to creep in and our ego takes over and before we know it, we have created a negative influence that could have been prevented.

What if we as a collective society agreed that our focus no matter what is going to be respect and how we give it and earn it? How would that look if we tried to understand the need for our differences instead of focusing on the differences? Can you even imagine what that would look like? Not long ago at one of the organizations where I worked, we had many challenges and did not have a great reputation when it came to dealing with folks both internally and externally. While doing leadership training at the beginning of the year I challenged the folks to focus on respect for a few months instead of complaining and griping about everything and blaming everything on someone else our goal was to respect each other internally. As you can imagine we had pushback from some folks at first, it is much easier to blame than problem-solve. What we ended up accomplishing was egos were set aside and we started looking at each other as a team that needed each other instead of despising each other. By simply changing our internal behavior of disrespecting each other to respect it translated to our customer service and interactions externally.

There is no way you can create an atmosphere of respect and teamwork that allows you to close some gaps without checking your ego at the door, no matter what. Without a doubt, this is easier said than done sometimes. There are folks out there who want to continue to create the divide because it simply fits their agenda and they never have to look at their own contribution, positive or negative. Most who do not want to change or self-reflect on things are usually the ones who are creating the issues and will continue to do so unless we make a more conscious effort to bring folks together.

How do we lead ourselves to a more positive outcome in our influence on others? Understand that differing perspectives are necessary, we are all different for a reason, and even though we can be like-minded, we need variety. We must find a way to self-reflect as needed to determine what our ego is saying. If it is good, grow it more; if it's bad, change it for the better. We must find ways to keep our pride in check so as not to create a negative influence. Being confident or taking pride in ourselves is not inherently bad as long as we keep our ego in check and do not allow it to influence us negatively.

How do we connect with others to better understand them?

I believe we must ask questions to find common ground but also to understand each other. What are the needs of the folks that work with me and how can I make things better? If we do not ask, how do we know? Again, this means putting the needs of others before our own, which can be difficult at times. I will talk later about ways to make the things we talk about easier if we are just intentional and disciplined.

We must be aware of the contributions and role we are playing in either closing or growing the gap. We must make changes if we are growing it, we must find ways to make sure our ego does not hinder the building of a bridge that could transform the way we operate both at work and at home. As long as we do not lose that focus, we can find ways to work together instead of against each other.

Things we must do and learn!

- We must check our ego as needed!
- Remember it's not about you every time all the time.
- We must strive to not let our pride get in the way. Be proud, but humble, not arrogant.
- Strive to understand those around you so you can keep your ego under control.
- Get out of your own way!

Do not let your ego get in your way!

Foundation

If we are going to figure out how to close and then bridge the gap, we must spend some time talking about our foundation. Why is our foundation so important? Because that is where we build everything else from. If it's weak it will crumble at every challenge that comes our way. If we are mindful of how we build our foundation and make it strong it will stand firm when challenges come.

We must build a strong foundation in order to grow and learn who we are. How do we do that and what goes into our foundation formula? Where do we get the information/ingredients for our own unique foundation? Many of us were taught by our parents or other folks that we held in high regard. They tried to instill in us things that they believed were important for us to function successfully in society. They taught us about faith, family values, morals, character, respect, and a sense of pride. This was not an attempt to make us better than anyone else, just to give us a starting point to build and grow in our character. However, somewhere along the way, we lost our understanding of how important it is to maintain a strong foundation in a world full of challenges and temptations. In many ways, we lost sight of what our whole being was built on and from. So, without a doubt we have to pay closer attention to how we form our foundation and then how we maintain its strength and integrity.

For some of us, this was an easier process because we had family that built our foundation on trust and respect. For many, this was not and has not been a smooth process. Nor did some of you have any good role models growing up that ensured your success in establishing the right foundation to face both positives and negatives. Those who did not have family or close friends who provided this structure turned to other avenues for guidance, some good some bad. I firmly believe that one of the issues we face today in creating divides is caused by building our foundation based on negativity and chaos rather than positivity and order. When we as family and friends do not provide the proper guidance and one turns to other avenues, they are faced with much inconsistency in how foundations are built. Most people have had the opportunity to learn, but because we have done a poor job as a society of being positive, many turn to the wrong builders for their influence. This results in poor foundations and crumbling structures instead of strong healthy ones that can be built upon.

The key is we have to find positive role models and influences who want to send the right message and care about the folks they influence. Even though some of us did not have the influence of family or friends, hopefully, we learned some positive traits and at least can understand the need to build a strong foundation to withstand anything that comes our way. This is important so that we can stand for what we believe in and not waver when the challenges come, and they will come. This may look different for many of us, but we were given the basic understanding that we should have a strong faith and belief system. Some of you may be saying I missed this step altogether; I had no parents and no one who stepped up until much later in life. No worries, we are going to talk about the importance of moving forward and building a strong foundation. The reality is we must start somewhere to create the proper foundation. If you are getting a late start, it just means you must be more intentional and disciplined as you move forward.

As I look back and reflect, I realize that my foundation was rooted in faith in God and a strong family filled with love. Now that doesn't mean that everything was perfect, but the beginning of the foundation was formed. I was taught right from wrong and that it was my choice to establish my own system. I knew that there would be consequences for anything that I thought, spoke, or did. Here is where we have deviated as a society and allowed common practices to dictate poor, unstable foundations. We have forgotten the principle that we are responsible for everything we think, say, or do. It's not someone else's fault it's our own and if it is negative there are consequences. We must stop allowing others to use excuses for their own choices and behaviors that are inherently bad and require them to take responsibility for their own actions.

Please do not misunderstand me here, I have not always made the right choices, but I have learned from my mistakes, and I am much better because of them. There is no way I could or can learn from my mistakes if I blame everyone else for the things that I think say or do. That is why it is important that we build our foundation in the proper way to withstand all challenges and issues that come our way.

For those of you who were not given a strong foundation or have not found people you can believe in, establishing a foundation creates a greater challenge! Each of us must find out what that belief system means for us. We must know what it means to have someone believe in us, or to rely on in every situation we encounter. In turn, we must also believe in ourselves and the strength of our foundation.

As leaders, we must be aware of certain things that allow us to understand our own belief system and what makes our foundation strong. This may be faith in God, your church, your life group, family, friends, and/or self. Yes, at some point we must have faith in ourselves. If you do not believe in you, why would someone else? Everyone's foundation might be a little different, but the concept remains the same. We must believe in something to have a strong foundation! Because we are not experts, we need to get help from others to build the best, strongest foundation possible.

Many people believe that when you talk about a belief system it only deals with religion. For me, that is only one facet of the system. However strong that system may be, it is still only a portion of what is needed. If you don't understand faith, religion, or God, then maybe you understand family and the need to understand, love, and believe in each other. This is nothing more than a support system to aid in creating your foundation. Or maybe you can understand the need for friends, and have a belief in friends that will stand by you in every situation. Friendships just like family must be strong, loving, and understanding. Find someone who can mentor you through understanding the process. Your goal is to use any or all of these to build the best foundation that will withstand time. The best models have faith, family, friends, with self-added to make it an even stronger foundation.

If you have not already you must start somewhere to understand your system, and how do you want your

FOUNDATION

foundation to develop? The stronger your foundation the better you become. Only you can decide what your foundation is built on: those discussed are an example of what I have used to build my foundation. Your starting point and everyone else's should be this: You have to believe in yourself and your capabilities!

>
>
> "BEGIN TODAY TO BELIEVE IN YOURSELF, START SELF-REFLECTING ON WHO YOU ARE CURRENTLY AND WHO YOU WANT TO BE."
>
> -Earl Morrison

No matter what or how strong your foundation is, your beliefs and character will be challenged. You will be challenged, sometimes daily! It can often feel as though the challenges just keep coming. If you don't have a strong foundation, you will not be able to take a stand. You will be easily influenced if your foundation is shaky and weak. If it is strong, you won't be easily influenced or swayed. If you lack any or all three, faith, family, and friends (4 with self), I suggest you start now to cultivate at least one and eventually all of them. Surround yourself with the right people of high character that want to see you succeed. Allow them to pour into you and help you establish the right formula for your foundation. Find people who truly care about you and want you to be the best you can be. Find at least one person to invest in you and mentor you!

At some point, we must take a hard look in the mirror and determine if our foundation is built on shaky ground or solid, stable ground. If we find that we have some needed repairs in our foundation, then we have work to do to make it stable again. If we find that we are in great condition, we must make sure we maintain its strength. Either way, we must always understand our foundation formula, what keeps it strong, and what may possibly weaken it. If we can figure out our own foundation formula, we can begin to understand the gaps created in life and how to decrease them or build a bridge to overcome them!

For those who may need or want a little help developing the right formula, here is mine:

- A strong faith-based belief that God is in control, and He will help you.

- Your family is there for you, but you must ask them, and they will help you. (Most of the time)
- A strong group of like-minded friends that will hold you accountable. Don't be afraid to quit or change friends. Change your influence as needed!
- Strong mentors in your life who will hold you accountable and want you to succeed.
- Surround yourself with positive influences and always keep your head held high.

Things we must do and learn!

- We must examine our current foundation and determine the shape it is in currently.
- We must make sure the things we build our foundation with are making it strong!
- We must allow others to help us build a strong foundation.
- Surround yourself with the right people.
- Hold yourself to the right foundation formula.
- Pray as needed, and you will need it.
- Make repairs as needed. Do not wait too long.
- Stay strong, be courageous!

We must have a strong foundation because it's the beginning of everything else we build. If we are going to bridge the gap our foundations must be strong and stable!

Character

As we discussed earlier, character is huge when it comes to having the ability to close the gap. Remember there are so many built-in gaps in our organizations, families, and society. Therefore, we must have a strong Godly, positive character in order to work with and understand each other. What does that mean? Simply put, it means we must do everything we can to first establish great character, and second we must protect it no matter what. "Never compromise your Character!"

I believe character and morals are two things that everyone wants to leave as their legacy, positively. But we must ask ourselves do we really know what that even means? As I have researched and studied this, I have established the following:

- Character means the mental and moral qualities distinctive to an individual.
- Morals are a person's standard of behavior or beliefs concerning what is or is not acceptable for them to do.

CHARACTER

Just like building our foundation the right way, who and what shapes our character is just as important. So, what actually shapes our character? Most people set out to have good positive attributes that shape their character and who they are as individuals. Daily and sometimes several times a day, we encounter people and situations that will provide lessons to shape and build our character. The reality is that often those very people that are helping us to build our character are our biggest challenges. In each and every decision that is made, or situation we find ourselves involved in, we have the conscious choice to decide if we are going to allow it to build our character positively or strip it away negatively. Therein lies the problem if our ego or foundation is not in the right shape!

Many times, in these situations we find ourselves surrounded by the wrong people who don't have our best interests at heart or are in it for themselves. The truth is we have too many negative influences as opposed to positive influences in our inner circle. This is why we must always be on our toes and constantly guard our character so that we can stand firm no matter what comes our way. Many times when we think these folks are in our corner they are not. No matter what, be on guard!

How can this be overcome? Each of us needs to figure out what character means to us. It may be very similar to what I provided but it could be slightly different only because we are each unique in our own way. This step is a must if we want to mind the gap and stand for our beliefs. There are several things that I believe are associated with true character: integrity, honor, trustworthiness, conscientiousness, sincerity, commitment, concern, and ethics to name a few. You certainly add to or take away from this list, but you get the gist of what goes into character. Nothing is more important than your character and the legacy you leave for others to follow. Again, this is why is so important to understand your level of influence.

You must decide what you are willing to accept as morally right so that you can continue to maintain your true character and preserve who you are. You are the one who is responsible for what you think, say, or do, so the choice is always yours! If you ever begin to compromise your character, it becomes easier and easier to fall into the trap of that compromise! Once this happens folks can become relentless in trying to challenge you and your character. There is no doubt in my mind that your character will be challenged more than once throughout your lifetime, sometimes you will fail, I have for sure. Understanding that we are going to fail is part of the battle, we are not perfect. However, that is why it is so important that we establish our own true character and do not rely on what someone else thinks or does. A hard lesson sometimes

CHARACTER

that can take a while to learn, it took me a while, and I needed to reduce the number of failures that I encountered. I realized that I needed to take a hard look at myself and what contribution I was making in building or tearing down my own character and morals. Once I was married and began having children, I realized what this meant. It's not about me, it's about the level of influence that I have and how I am leading everyone who is watching me up close and from afar.

Once we have established who we are and the character and morals we want to be remembered for, we must develop a method to preserve that character. Here are some things that I have learned along the way, with lots of lumps and failures. Preserving my character means I must hold myself accountable even if no one else does. I must allow others to hold me accountable and understand there are consequences when we get it wrong. I must spend time on self-refection as needed. It will be needed and is an ongoing process. Learn from my mistakes even when it can be a hard lesson. Accept responsibility for our own thoughts, speech, and actions. It is not everyone else's fault! Establish what character means to me and never compromise my character.

Are you surrounding yourself with the right people to challenge you to achieve, maintain, or develop the positive character and morals you want? I ask this question because we should not be trying to do any of this by ourselves, we must allow others to help us no matter how difficult. We must take a close look at our friends, family, peers, community leaders, coaches, and mentors and determine if any or all of these are growing us positively or stripping us away negatively. Don't forget that we should make changes in any of these that we can to establish the positive character we want to be remembered for with our legacy. As you self-reflect ask yourself, who am I allowing to control my character and what changes if any do I need to make?

The next thing we should try to understand is what kind of things challenge our character. I suggest you actually spend some time thinking about this and work hard to determine what poses a challenge for you. You may need to talk this through with someone else. I have found that when I talk to other people it helps me put things in perspective because I realize it's not just me that faces these challenges. Let me share a few things that challenge my character and possibly yours as well. Things that make it difficult to maintain our character: Toxic people and/or a toxic environment, negative influences, unexpected challenges and/or obstacles, temptation from anything and everything that could make it difficult to maintain your character. For me, the major challenge has always been toxic people in a toxic environment. Unfortunately, I have had the opportunity to experience both throughout my lifetime. It can be easier if you only have a few or a single toxic person but combine that with a toxic environment, and it is very challenging. This is when we have to be very intentional to keep ourselves healthy and maintain our character no matter what!

THINGS YOU MUST LEARN:

- Maintaining your character never stops, you can never rest easy.

- There are always going to be temptations (challenges) that challenge your character and who you are.

- Once you compromise your character, it is easier to continue to compromise your behavior.

- Never compromise your character!

If we want to close the gap, we must establish and maintain a positive mindset and character that does not falter when challenged!

Leadership

Leadership can be so confusing, speaking about something that has gaps. I believe that part of the problem is that we tend to try and find one size that fits all. There is no way that we can determine one style of leadership that fits every situation or person. I think this is often confusing because we always try to fit everything perfectly into the boxes and squares, we have created. Just look at how many different styles of leaders and leadership there are out there. How many different surveys or character tests are there that we use to determine exactly who we are as leaders? The reality of it is that none of them are 100% dead on determining who we really are as leaders. I think part of the reason this is so difficult is that leadership and leading people is situational. What style or behaviors you use are determined by the timing, facts, experience, situation, and desired outcome at the time it is needed.

I am by nature a servant leader. Many of us want to think of ourselves as a servant leader because most of us do the things we do to make things better for someone else. We love everything that being a servant leader stands for and strive to achieve that daily. I would be remiss if I just left it at that and didn't give you the rest of the story. Even though I am a servant leader there have been plenty of time where I had to be a dictator because time or the situation didn't allow me to be democratic. Those that are leaders that have been in some difficult situations that call for action know exactly what I mean. Sometimes I don't need to debate, just trust and respect that I know what I am doing and that I will make the best decision for the desired outcome at hand. There are times when the best way is to be democratic and allow input and feedback, if you can get it. But everyone must understand that someone has to make decisions, sometimes hard decisions, and each person needs to understand their role on the team.

I am a hands-on person; I walk around and observe. This is not to do everything or undermine anyone, but to learn what each person does and the value each person brings to the team. This is the process of striving to understand the people and the organization so we can work together to achieve the desired outcome or goal. This is also a way to establish and understand the role each person has for the team and the organization. How do we determine any of this if we are not making an effort to understand each other and work together as a team? How are we closing the gap in leadership if we are not working together to better understand each other. In my opinion there is no perfect leadership model that fits every situation. Therefore, we must be mindful to strive to understand who we are as leaders and whom we are leading.

Another issue in leadership and leading is the often misunderstood and confused interpretation of leading and managing. We often say we know the difference between the two, but when asked we rarely are actually separating them. This can cause much confusion since we try to use them interchangeably! If we don't fully understand the difference, then we are definitely creating gaps in leadership due to our lack of understanding.

Leading vs. Managing

Often people confuse these two and think they are the same. Even though everyone always says they know the difference, many do not. This is based on how this has been perceived over the years. The problem is that many just go with it because they do not know any difference. That is why it is so key that we understand the difference and how that plays into our own understanding of leadership.

This has been a longstanding debate across all disciplines and industries everywhere. Many people call leaders "managers" in their organization and think that managers are also "leaders". This can be very confusing because of the way we use these terms interchangeably for each other. When this occurs, it becomes very misleading because they are not the same! However, as I stated earlier, we often use them interchangeably like they are the same because we do not know better. This is not anyone's fault it just happens when we get caught up in a certain way of doing things or a belief about something without fact or willingness to learn different. Evet leader and head of an organization or group must make it a priority to teach and allow the organization or group to learn and understand the difference and the need for both.

I teach everyone that the easiest way to understand the difference is that leaders are concerned about the people. Managers are concerned about the process. Leaders will always have management responsibility, but managers may not always be leaders or have that responsibility! Leaders understand both leading and managing within an organization. They will guide, mentor, teach, train, coach, and pave the way. They set the example, the vision and the course! Leaders cast a vision for the organization. (change) They motivate and inspire others to work towards the vision. They encourage, inspire, mentor, develop and guide people to overcome challenges to accomplish the vision.

Leadership

- Leaders want their people to succeed and mentor them to accomplish their goals.

- Leaders want things to be managed such as assets, resources, systems, programs, operations, projects, productivity, etc.

- Leaders focus more on the people who manage things and not the things.

- Leaders want satisfaction (success) for the people and the process to have an effective and efficient organization.

"Leadership is a matter of having people look at you and gain confidence, seeing how you react. If you're in control, they're in control."
~Tom Landry

"Effective leaders of people are almost always effective managers of things. However, effective managers are not always effective leaders."
~Mike Ettore
(Trust-based Leadership: Marine Corps Leadership Concepts for Today's Business Leaders)

Managers have management responsibility, but managers may not always be leaders or have that responsibility! They understand processes and plans, keep things moving, check the boxes, they accomplish the goals. Managers follow the course! Managers focus on the things: assets, resources, systems, programs, operations, projects, productivity, effort, etc. They want satisfaction (success) from the process not the people. Managers set out to achieve organizational goals. They are critical in getting things done but focus more on that than the people doing the work. This does not mean that they are not needed or not important, their focus is just different.

I think this is where some confusion comes from because they are important, and we sometimes tend to worry more about the processes or tasks than the people that help us accomplish them. Therefore, we create an issue because when complete or accomplish a task or mission we get too focused on that success and forget the people that made it a success. Without the people the task or mission does not get accomplished. This is why we must change our thinking and focus to better understand leading verses managing, so we do not forget about the people that made us successful!

If we took some time to break down the characteristics of a leader, we could come up with lots of things that would describe a leader. Here are a few that I often use in this discussion: Character, Charisma, Commitment,

CLOSING THE GAP BY BUILDING BRIDGES FOR ORGANIZATIONAL AND PERSONAL SUCCESS!

Communication, Competence, Courage, Discernment, Focus, Generosity, Initiative, Listening, Passion, Positive Attitude, Problem Solving, Relationships, Responsibility, Security, Self-Discipline, Servanthood, Teachability, Vision, and Accountable, just to name a few. There are many folks out there that have written books about these as well. One of my favorites is John Maxwell who without a doubt is the leadership guru of our time. I love his book "The 21 Indispensable Qualities of a Leader."

In turn of we break down the characteristics of a manager, we would come up with several to describe a manager. Here are a few that I use in this discussion: Communication, Organization, Delegation, Problem Solving, Strategic Thinking, Planning, Responsible, Feedback, Knowledge, Technical skills, Stress Management, and Coordinator to name a few.

Of course, some of these can be used interchangeably which is why the confusion exists. However, we are careful, and we break them down we can clearly see that the leader is people oriented and the manager is process focused. Leaders make good managers but not all managers make good leaders! If we are going to be able to bridge the gap, we must ask ourselves some very critical questions.

Are you a leader or a manager? I know this can be daunting but if we want to be better and close this gap, we must take the step and find out before it is too late.

Get some help to understand, learn who you are as a person and a leader. Know your strengths and weaknesses and be accountable no matter what you learn.

What do your people think? Would they say leader, manager, or both? Please do not shy away from asking these critical questions. It will only make you better. Take some time to understand your people and take some time to help them understand you and your style of leading. Be accountable, be consistent in good times and bad, and allow them time to understand and learn who you are and who they are. Learn to grow together.

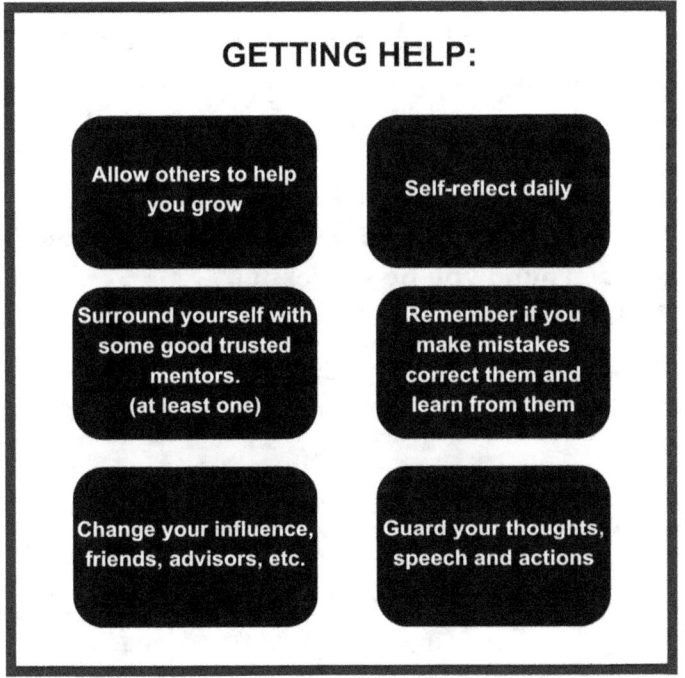

Things we must do and learn!

- We must understand that one size does not fit all.
- Leadership is very situational, and you may use more than one style.
- Leadership is based on the desired outcome.
- We must understand the difference between leading and managing.
- We must strive to understand who we are as leaders and understand those we lead.
- You must determine if you have been leading or managing.
- We must become better leaders if that is our mission.
- Everyone is at least a leader of one!
- Would you follow You?

"As a leader, it is your responsibility to help those around you be successful."
Earl Morrison

Generational

When we talk about gaps generational is the one that gets discussed most often. Whatever generation we find ourselves in, is the one we tend to relate to most. However, there are lots of things that go into this. Let's take a look at the different generations and see if we can help close the gap in understanding each one and the value brought by all.

Greatest Generation (Born 1901-1927): Came of age in an era of rapidly innovating technology, including the telephone, radio, and television, and war such as World War I! They are known for their ability to adapt and thrive in crisis and are celebrated for leaving the world better than they found it. Known as hard workers who never gave up no matter what!

Silent Generation (Born 1928-1945): Known as traditionalists, the Silent Generation were small in number due to low birthrates in the 1920s and 1930s and were generally raised as kids to be seen and not heard, hence their name (coined by Time in a 1951 essay). Like the Greatest Generation, they survived the Great

Depression and were born during periods of war such as World War II. Generally opposed wars such as Korea and Vietnam.

Baby Boomers (Born 1946-1964): Named due to the "baby boom" that followed World War II. There are 76 million Baby Boomers. Known for their post-World War II optimism, Baby Boomers were largely shaped by the Cold War, Vietnam War, and Civil Rights, hippie, and yuppie movements. Boomers generally value interpersonal communication and are largely fluent with technology. Boomers are regarded as driven, especially financially, to the point of often being criticized as greedy. They were one of the first generations to popularize the "live to work" lifestyle, and there may be a reason for that that they may not have expected during their youth: Social Security and Medicare may not be able to support them in retirement because there are simply so many of them. Probably the most talked about and how they shaped the workforce.

Gen X (1965-1980) Me: Often referred to as a forgotten generation. They had the highest rate of divorced parents of any generation. Gen Xers are more focused on work-life balance than their workaholic Boomer parents because they were often "latch-key kids." Though sometimes accused of being lazy and cynical, Gen X is largely entrepreneurial, and one of the last generations not to be saddled with crippling student loan debt. We grew up during several historical events that defined and shaped Gen X, including The end of the Cold War, Ronald Reagan's laissez-faire economics and recession, the crack and AIDS epidemics, and the rise of home computing and the internet. Gen Xers were also at the rise of informality at the office, something generations that followed have also adopted.

Millennials (1981-1995): Called out for technology addiction and alleged narcissism, but there's much more to them than their devices and Instagram feeds. Also known as Generation Y, millennials have lived through two major recessions, countless mass shootings, racial and civil unrest, 9/11, and the two longest wars in American history (Iraq and Afghanistan). Time called them entitled and bratty, labeling them the "me, me, me generation." This can at least partially be attributed to millennials having created and proliferated social media. Remember MySpace? Millennials are also the generation most likely to suffer from and seek help for mental illnesses and disorders like depression and anxiety, due in no small part to the immense pressure to succeed like prior generations as well as the lack of economic opportunities to do so. Millennials are the first generation to have higher rates of both unemployment and student loan debt than preceding generations. As an age group, Millennials are apprehensive about homeownership owing to a lack of financial stability and have largely delayed marriage and children for the same reason.

Gen Z (1996-2015): Are the first truly digital native generation, with many receiving their first phone before 11 years old. More social media savvy than their millennial peers, Gen Z folks are more aware of social justice and political issues than many of their older generations were at the same age, largely due to their heavy social media use. Studies have shown that Gen Z folks possess a great deal of emotional intelligence compared to elder generations and are more likely to partake in activism. Because Gen Z is still so young, however, there isn't a ton of data on them just yet—but we're looking forward to how they'll make their mark. Three of my kids fall into this generation. These are the newest members of society who are now entering the workforce, which brings on even more challenges.

As we look at all of the generations and where we and those we have encountered fall into, it is important to look a little closer at why the gaps are there. What I mean is that each of these three key things plays a role in how we look at and experience each person and their distinctive generation. These three things are age, experience, and stage in life. Part of the reason I believe we struggle so much with this is the gaps that are built in due to each of these.

Why are each of these such huge factors in how we interact with each other? The biggest is the level of maturity and the things that were instilled in each of us due to the influence of our generations. How does an older person who is close to or entering retirement connect with a teenager, twentysomething, or middle-aged person? First, we must understand the stages of life that each of us is in at the time of our interactions. We see things differently because our priorities change during stages in life. What may seem important as a youngster may not be of the same importance as I grow older and wiser. I may not think as strongly about retirement at a younger age as I will when I grow older. To better understand each other and the generational differences we must learn as much as we can about the individual and not place everyone in the category because of when they were born.

We must find ways to understand the value that each of us brings to the table and stop automatically labeling one another. If we can better understand where each person is in their stage of life, we can better relate to each other. Therefore, we need to strive to close the gaps by opening our minds and learning about the folks that are entering our organizations. If we want to get better at bridging the gap, we must make sure that we teach our people what we need them to know and understand about who we are as individuals and as an organization. We must show them value and what everyone brings to the table.

CLOSING THE GAP BY BUILDING BRIDGES FOR ORGANIZATIONAL AND PERSONAL SUCCESS!

To close or bridge the gap everyone must understand where they fall in their stage of life both personally and professionally. Each of us must understand what our contribution is to the organization and each situation we may encounter. What role are we playing in understanding differences (gaps) and are we willing to learn both our weaknesses and strengths when encountering people outside of our own generation, experience level, and stage in life? This must be part of growth and development as we learn to understand and close the gaps to make ourselves better as individuals, and leaders and improve our organizations. We can bridge these gaps if we are intentional and disciplined to understand that we must provide an environment where we can all adapt to each other's strengths and weaknesses while growing, learning, and developing together. We must understand our contribution in either closing/bridging the gap or causing it to get wider!

Things we must do and learn!

- We must understand the differences in our generations.
- Differences are caused by age, experience, knowledge, and stage in life.
- We must know where we are in our own stage of life.

- We must strive to understand why these gaps exist.
- We must work to close the gaps that can be closed.
- We must work together to bridge the gaps that cannot be closed.
- Mind the Gap! It could mean the success or failure of any individual or organization!

If we do not learn to better understand each other then the gap will just continue to grow!

Communication

Honestly, I think you could probably write a whole book on communication, and many have, I know John Maxwell has just written one, but I have not read it yet. Maybe if he reads mine, I will read his (lol)!

There is no doubt that we have a huge gap in our communication and communication styles almost as much as our generation gaps if not more in some instances. I believe the best way to start to close this gap is to try and understand what communication is and why we use it daily and several times daily throughout our lifetime. The better we understand communication the better we can communicate with each other! We must strive to become efficient and effective in our communication no matter where we are or what we are trying to communicate. "Poor communication, miscommunication, and lack of communication are detrimental to the proficiency of any organization!" These are detrimental to any relationship or partnership!

What does communication even mean? If you asked several people, you would most likely get several different

COMMUNICATION

answers based on their understanding. Communication is a process by which information is exchanged between individuals through a common system of symbols, signs, or behavior, an exchange of information. A way to build personal rapport, information communicated: transmitted or conveyed, a verbal or written message.

What are communications? A system (telephone, computer) for transmitting or exchanging information, a system for expressing ideas effectively (speech), the transmission of information (print, telecommunication), an act or instance of transmitting.

Now that we have an idea of what communication is and the systems used let's explore the ways in which we communicate. There are many ways we communicate or send messages; some we are very aware of and some not so much. We communicate through speech, words, conversation, written words, emails, texts etc. Then there are the very generational methods of social media: Facebook, Instagram, Twitter, etc. And then the ones that some people are not aware of how they impact their communication efforts. These are body language, signs, behaviors, attitudes, actions, demeanor, etc. This last group is the ones that get most of us in trouble because we are not very aware of our own communication styles and efforts! They always give us away if we are communicating in person and the speech does not match the body language or expressions!

CLOSING THE GAP BY BUILDING BRIDGES FOR ORGANIZATIONAL AND PERSONAL SUCCESS!

The next question is why do we communicate? What is our goal in any or all of our communications? What is our desired outcome? At a minimum, we use communications to share information. Any leader or person would do this to create a vision, expressing ideas, thoughts, and concerns, especially entering a new organization or an established one to effect change. We use communication to gain buy-in, ownership, credibility, validity, support, etc. We use communication to build teamwork, efficiency, effectiveness, accountability, etc., throughout the organization or group we are involved with, and even with family and friends. Other reasons we communicate are to gain trust, create transparency, build relationships/partnerships, convey our goals, mission, etc. to stakeholders, and express ourselves.

The last thing to help us better understand communication and why there are gaps is communication challenges. This is going to be similar for many of us but also very unique based on our own strengths and weaknesses of communication. Here are a few things I like to discuss in my classes. Most of us want to build trust and what better way than the ability to communicate effectively? If we can't communicate effectively, it will most likely create mistrust and a lack of respect. A major challenge for any leader of a people, or an organization, is building transparency vs. secrecy or misinformation. In many of the organizations where I have worked if it was not communicated someone would fill in the gaps and it usually led to falsehoods or half-truths. In turn, it created avenues for gossip or misconstrued conversations or information, definitely a challenge.

Even when we do well in our communication other challenges arise such as consistency of communication and information. Just when we think we are good at it or have it figured out, we realize we now have to maintain that level no matter what is happening or when it happens. Within these challenges, we must also contend with negative or toxic individuals who sow internal discord and foster a toxic atmosphere. Those are all challenges that can derail the most well-intended and informed communications if we allow them to happen.

Last but certainly not least is differing communication styles. This can be a huge challenge because everyone receives our communications differently. A loud tone while unintended may cause anxiety to those that don't like that style. A direct and to-the-point style can cause folks to take things personally because it feels that way when someone is in front of us. I believe that this is an area where we must learn as much as we can about the folks we are communicating with and adapt to what works best for them. Yes, this is much easier said than done at times. However, we must make the effort if we want to bridge the gap and better understand each other.

CLOSING THE GAP BY BUILDING BRIDGES FOR ORGANIZATIONAL AND PERSONAL SUCCESS!

Communication plays such a huge role in everything we do and everything we are about. This is another area where we must pay close attention to our generations and the gaps in how we share information and the style in which we share it. There are so many ways we put out information in today's world. There is face-to-face, my preferred way in challenging situations or very important information. We have our instant access email that gets information out to the masses and is needed but often misunderstood or misinterpreted due to lack of emotion and visual aid of body language and expressions. Then there is the text message which offers personal connection and intimacy. That is unless you are a group texter and always reply to all! We still have the written letter or note as well for the professional or the intimate message from time to time. Each person has their own likes and dislikes for what type of communication they prefer. I believe each situation and ensuing message will determine what style to use depending on how or what I want to be construed.

One of the things I have learned over the last several years is that we must be intentional in making sure we are teaching the younger generations face-to-face communication. I believe I can speak with a little bit of expertise here with three teenagers who fit this category. They have grown up in an instant-access and technology-led world when it comes to communication. They are well-versed in texting, social media, and even the occasional phone call at times. What they are not very well versed in is face-to-face communication. They lack the interpersonal skills to interact socially with folks in a live environment unless someone has been intentional about teaching them. Now, if you or your children do not fit this do not get mad at me, I am just pointing out what I have experienced and learned through my own interactions and teaching. Without fail it has been brought up in my classes and the older more experienced folks always want to blame the younger folks. This always gives me the opportunity to point out that we must be intentional and disciplined when teaching and acclimating folks to our environment and culture when it comes to communication. They can't and won't communicate well if we do not recognize this and teach them and us to be better in all avenues of communication.

To bridge or close the communication gap we must strive to understand what communication means and why we use it. We must know our communication style and our challenges to get better and understand each other both internally and externally. If you do some research over 70% of our communications are misunderstood, or the wrong message was received. There are many factors that could cause this such as distractions, I always bring up cell phones here, because we are constantly looking at and or responding to an email, text message, or phone call no matter the environment or venue we find ourselves. Often the message is not heard or partially heard, remember many of us listen to answers not to understand. Sometimes we just reject the information, again this can be for many reasons both personal and perceived.

Another thing to consider in closing the communication gap is conversation traps. Those well-intended conversations where someone heard something wrong, or we said a little too much and sent the wrong impression. Every leader must be aware of the need for employees and folks who fall within their level of influence to connect with them in some way. This means there are no idle conversations, you must be on guard to not make things worse than the already built-in challenges of communication. We must be aware of whom we are communicating with and the messages we are sending constantly. Are you sending the right message and are you having the right kind of conversation that enhances your communications not hinder them?

COMMUNICATION

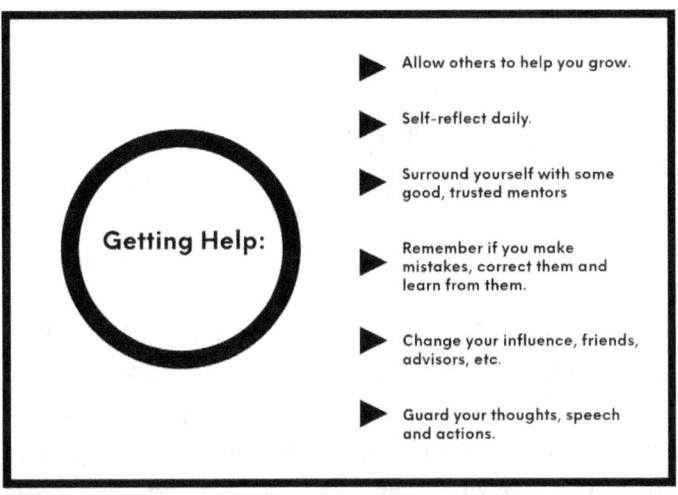

- Allow others to help you grow.
- Self-reflect daily.
- Surround yourself with some good, trusted mentors
- Remember if you make mistakes, correct them and learn from them.
- Change your influence, friends, advisors, etc.
- Guard your thoughts, speech and actions.

Things You Must Do and Learn:

- Learn as much as you can about the communication/conversation challanges you face and make changes as needed.
- Seek to understand your folks (others) first and then to be understood. (Covey)
- Keep the desired outcome in mind in all conversations and communications.
- Be accountable for you thoughts, speech and actions.

If we are going to close the communication gap or bridge the gap, we must be intentional and disciplined to be better and understand those we communicate with and then understand our own communication style and challenges!

Mental Health

This is one of those topics that we should have been talking about long before now. Even today it seems like it is still one that people tend to shy away from or keep private. Not that our mental health isn't a private issue, it's just that it is okay to talk about it. Yeah, what a concept that we talk about our mental health with others, maybe even our co-workers from time to time. At a minimum, we should have someone that we can talk about everything to and know that they are listening and not judging.

I firmly believe that we created this stigma that if we had to talk to someone about our mental health then we had real issues. The crazy thing is many of us are the same way about our physical health. We always think we can figure it out on our own even though most of us have proven we can't. Now don't get me wrong, I realize sometimes we can treat our signs and symptoms from medical issues with over-the-counter remedies or Band-Aids. I think our mental issues are not that simple and when I say issues, I simply mean the things that each of us deal with daily. I feel that we often do not even realize the things we encounter have such a major impact on how we deal with things, how we react or overreact, how we carry ourselves, or how we act.

For most of us when we entered adulthood and/or the workforce we never really thought that the very things we do every day could play a huge role in our own mindset and attitude. Some thought how could this be an issue when it's what I love to do? We may even have the thought that there is no way it could be job or work-related. Okay, so take a little time and do some self-reflecting on your own mindset. What are your stressors, triggers, those things that tend to push your buttons? These can cause many emotions and reactions in all of us, it's not necessarily that you have them, it's how long you spend in those emotions or reactions. If you are one of those folks who seem to be trapped in them, then you need to allow someone to help you. I know this is not an easy task, but it will be very beneficial.

You see we generally want to keep most things in instead of finding an avenue to vent, gripe, or even complain. Those are all healthy and much needed if done in the right way and in the correct venue. When we can't find a release, we start allowing those emotions of anxiety, frustration, failure, fear, mistrust, anger, and criticism, and we become cynical and jaded no matter what happens. I know I have been here myself, and I did not realize the damage I was doing not only to myself but to those around me. Remember your level of influence? It's important that you do not forget how great your level of influence may be. Just so no one misunderstands me or gets confused I am not a doctor so I'm not talking about real deep-rooted mental illness here, that is a whole other subject. I am merely trying to point out the importance of making sure that in our day-to-day lives whether we are at work or home we are aware of the things that cause us to become drained, tired, frustrated, confused, angry, frustrated, etc.

Why do I want you to be aware of these and what does that have to do with closing the gap? Throughout my career, I have been involved in organizations that are service-oriented. Many of you are as well. Most of us would say we got into the industry to help others to make a difference and serve. However, those are the very things that cause much of our negative or detrimental mindsets. I have spent the last twenty-three years in law enforcement, and twenty-nine in the criminal justice field. For the most part, especially early on we have done a poor job of taking care of ourselves mentally and maintaining a positive mindset throughout our careers. Why is a great question, but I really think it is because we allowed this to be the normal way of operations. Partially because we didn't know any better and then when we did many created such a stigma about talking about our feelings, we labeled anyone that didn't conform to the old way.

Isn't that par for the course? We want folks to do things the right way and take care of themselves and instead of helping them we label them and create a bigger roadblock for them and others. I can say with 100% surety we are much better than we used to be at this. We just can't stop because we are better, we must continue to strive to learn as much as we can about our issues and triggers and continue to get help. As administrators and leaders, we must make this a priority to allow our folks to get the much-needed help to maintain a healthy mindset. I also believe we are getting better at helping our veterans as well as all first responders in understanding these issues and getting help to cope with them. Just think about the things that you as a regular tax-paying citizen encounter throughout your day and lifetime. Now think about the kind of things that our military, police officers, firemen, and first responders encounter daily and in their lifetime. There are several folks out there who have written some books and do seminars and talks that help both the first responder and military veteran.

Let's talk about one of the biggest contributors to this, our own attitude. I firmly believe that your attitude is your responsibility. It's so important that I wrote about this in my first book "Leadership Lessons Learned," as well as "Mentoring for Life." I also teach a whole module on "Your Attitude; Your Responsibility."

The reason this is so important to understand is we often experience all the things I have mentioned and then we blame it on our work, friends, other people, spouses, etc. It's always everyone else's fault and not my own. "You and only you can set the tone for your attitude." It is your choice how you go through each situation! Maybe you can relate to some of the things we talk about in class. Think about some of these things and reflect on what your behavior was when this was you: Maybe you encounter someone you don't like, or you are greeted by your boss who doesn't appreciate you. What if you get attacked because of a decision you made? It could even feel personal because you don't get along with the individual who attacked you this morning. That attack could have been a simple good morning, but we were already in a bad mood. What if you or someone else got up on the wrong side of the bed?

Just so everyone understands the need to self-reflect here, I always say that everyone knows someone who will pop into your head when thinking about a negative behavior or mindset. I always caution that if you can't think of anyone then it is probably you! Yeah, I know that hurts but it's what you need to hear, you could be the negative, toxic, mind-altering, and attitude-setting

MENTAL HEALTH

person that is creating the same for someone else. I don't think this is where most people want to be!

Because of all those scenarios we decide, well I want to be mad and angry, and I might even do or say something that conveys that. Sometimes this becomes our normal behavior every day. We have the mindset of: You made me mad and I'm going to take it out on everyone else that I encounter for the rest of today and maybe even tomorrow. The next thing we know we have created a culture of negativity and the environment around us becomes toxic. Before we know it that is how we are perceived both as an individual and as an organization. Usually, at this point, everyone starts blaming everything on everyone else and the place where you work. Instead of not allowing ourselves to go there we find and create excuse after excuse to justify the behavior and attitude. When we look closely, we realize what just happened in those scenarios and across the days, weeks, months, and even years. Yep, you just allowed someone else to dictate how your day is going to be, maybe even your week, month, or year! We must realize that we allowed someone else to set the tone for our attitude. I am no longer in control of my own attitude and demeanor. I am possibly the tone setter for someone else's attitude and it's not positive.

I know it's easier to go with the angry, upset attitude where I can easily justify my actions based on my earlier encounter with my boss or employee. Sure, you can go with that attitude and allow someone else to dictate your attitude. But who gives anyone else the right to dictate who we are and how we respond? Well to be honest only you give this ability to others. Why do we so often choose to let others get us down, manipulate us with negativity, or force us into bad attitudes? We feel angered, hurt, confused, or even betrayed. We want others to feel our pain as well. It really doesn't matter what the situation was, we want justice, and we want as many people as we can to feel what we feel. You know the old saying: misery loves company!

So why can't we do that in a positive way? Why can't we go forward with a positive, happy, healthy attitude and response? "Because we want to feel vindicated or justified, so we react in that way to garner a response that proves we were right from the onset." This plays into the mindset that it's not my fault, it's everyone else's. Who can I blame because it's easier than taking responsibility for myself? How do we avoid this situation and strive to get better? We avoid this by self-reflection and discipline, to be true to ourselves and who we are as an individual. We must take control of our own attitudes and destiny and set the tone for our own attitude. We must remember that "You and only you can set the tone for your attitude!" Don't allow anyone to control who you are

MENTAL HEALTH

and who you want to be, look for positive mentors and examples to follow.

- Self-reflect.
- Discipline yourself.
- Find at least one Mentor.
- Find some trusted advisors of high character.
- Be positive!

Why do we allow others to control our attitude or emotions?

- We are emotionally vulnerable, but we do not want anyone to know.
- We are focused on other things/distracted, which happens to all of us.
- We want to fit in and go with the flow, go along to get along.
- It helps us blame others and deflect responsibility!
- It requires effort and self-reflection to remain positive!
- It's easier than being accountable for our own thoughts, speech, or actions.
- I put my trust in the wrong people to be honest with me, not a great feeling at all.
- I don't care about myself, others, or how I am perceived.
- Nobody cares! It just feels that way sometimes and we play into it too often.
- This place is toxic anyway so why does it matter?

What steps do you need to take daily to set the tone for your attitude?

- Self-reflect daily and be prepared, this must become a priority!
- Remain positive no matter what, stay strong.
- Stop blaming others and accept responsibility for your own thoughts, speech, and actions.
- Find a trusted colleague to help keep my attitude/emotions in check. They will tell you what you need to hear not always what you want to hear.
- Be accountable for my own actions!
- Treat others the way you want to be treated!
- Don't be the person that makes it toxic.
- Be the change you want to see.
- Hit the reset button as often as needed.

Things we must do and learn!

- We must understand the need for a positive healthy mindset.
- Self-reflect as needed to keep ourselves healthy.
- We must be intentional and disciplined.
- We must make mental health, mindset, and attitude a priority as individuals and organizations.

MENTAL HEALTH

If you really want to be mindful of the gap you must allow others to hold you accountable. You must surround yourself with good, trusted advisors, and find at least one Mentor. Ask for help, make changes as needed, embrace the changes, and bridge the gap.

Accountability

This is one of the hardest topics to talk about. Most of us would say we want accountability in our lives as well as our organization. However, many do not know what that means or how it is accomplished. This is due to our lack of establishing real standards and then actually practicing accountability in a firm, fair, and consistent manner. How do we practice accountability if we do not know the standard?

Now do not misunderstand me here I believe many out there have tried to establish some accountability in their lives as well as organizations. There are tons of models, examples, and folks that are setting the example for us to follow in a positive manner. However, there are as many or more out there who are trying so hard to sabotage a person or agency that they will forgo all accountability to make things easier for themselves. Unfortunately, just like many of you, I have experienced this in more than one organization where I have worked. It does not account for a very positive, pleasant place to work. In fact, it is usually very toxic and chaotic merely due to the lack of or inconsistency of accountability.

ACCOUNTABILITY

Do you ever just sit back and think about accountability and what it means? Not just the regular definition, but what does it mean for you as an individual and what does it mean for your group or organization? One of the major issues is our lack of understanding just what is meant by accountability. If we do not define this, then we will find ourselves all over the place because each person will try to determine what it means to them. Newsflash: we do not always get it right; we are usually trying to find a way to make it easier for ourselves. Do you ever sit back and say I wish someone would hold those people accountable for their actions? The things that those people do are bad, and nobody seems to care. How do they get away with it?

Here is what I have found; this sounds great when I consider accountability for others. But when it hits me, it becomes personal. So, what happens when you become the person that needs to be held accountable? Suddenly it feels so different, I have to be accountable for what I think, say, and do! I didn't sign up for that kind of accountability! This kind of response is why accountability is always so intriguing to me. We know that accountability is needed, but when it becomes personal, we become resistant. This resistance leads to inconsistency and a lack of real accountability throughout your organization.

CLOSING THE GAP BY BUILDING BRIDGES FOR ORGANIZATIONAL AND PERSONAL SUCCESS!

If you look at many organization preferences by employers and employees, they mostly all say they want accountability. This is part of many promotional processes or job postings looking for leaders or executives. Time and time again you will hear people complain that in their workplace or organization, there is no accountability. People get away with anything and everything. Our organization doesn't move forward because no one is held accountable for any of their actions. I once spent three months in a hiring process that focused on accountability, they even required a one-year game plan. Only to find out a short time later they were not ready for real change and accountability. It sounds good until you have to put in the work!

"People say they want accountability until they are the one held accountable." Earl Morrison

If we want to close the gap, we must understand what accountability means, both to us as individuals and as an organization or group. Accountability is nothing more than an obligation or willingness to accept responsibility or to account for one's actions. Do you mean I am responsible for my own thoughts, speech, and actions? Wow, if we actually put this into practice how would things be? If I am responsible for myself then I can't blame everyone and everything for what I think, say, or do! At some point along the way, we have gotten away from this practice of accountability and used it to excuse and allow certain behaviors that have only added to the lack or inconsistency of accountability.

Leaders are accountable for accountability.

I believe that accountability is important to the survival and success of any organization. If you want accountability within an organization, you must allow the leadership to perform a complete analysis of those within the organization. You must allow the person who has conducted the analysis to proceed with their assessment of the individuals and the organization. Both the leaders and the organization need to trust that this analysis and assessment has been done thoroughly and is based on the facts and situations presented to that person. This is key if we really want a firm, fair, and consistent level of accountability to allow the people and the organization to grow and develop together.

CLOSING THE GAP BY BUILDING BRIDGES FOR ORGANIZATIONAL AND PERSONAL SUCCESS!

Having accountability in your personal/private life is just as important as within an organization. You must truly understand what accountability means and how much it is needed. Accountability done correctly is never about anything personal between the person being held accountable and the person holding them accountable. However, the person being corrected usually makes it personal. We must get away from this and understand the need for accountability. Furthermore, we must understand what kind of family unit or organization we will have if we lack accountability. Accountability is in place for the good and betterment of the organization and individual. It provides an avenue for growth, development, and organization.

Accountability provides law and order and is the basis for correction and discipline. When accountability is lacking no one wins and individuals as well as the organization will suffer. We put this in place to be able to avoid chaos and toxicity. It builds responsibility, character, reliability, and credibility for both the individual and the organization. A look back throughout History will provide enough information to understand why we need accountability across the board.

I often talk about the fact that everyone has policies, procedures, or some form of guideline that provides the basis for accountability. I usually ask if anyone has a flow chart in their specific guideline. The answer is

ACCOUNTABILITY

always no, but it feels like there is one. I'm going to age myself a bit. Remember the old flowchart when we were working on computer programs or other projects? I even used a flow chart when performing sick calls in the Army. If it met a certain symptom or quality, it went in one direction, if it didn't' it went the other. Each one had very different results in the end. Unfortunately, this is how many feel when it's time for accountability. If we like you there is one result if we don't there is another that has many more consequences. You can even change the scenario if you are new, we hammer you if you have been here a while you get off easier. Look, I can't make that up, that is a fact and most of us have experienced accountability in that way.

Therein lies much of our problem when we talk about accountability. The lack thereof or inconsistency creates very confusing and toxic environments. These are hard to overcome when there is no accountability, no responsibility, and no consequence for oneself. Yes, with accountability there are consequences. The greater the issue the greater the consequence. If you do not like the consequence, then do not violate the issue.

If we ever want to close the gap, we must hold ourselves accountable and allow others to hold us accountable! If not, the gap just keeps getting bigger and bigger and our organizations become more and more dysfunctional and toxic.

Understanding and Accepting Accountability

- Don't make it personal!
- Accept responsiblity for your own actions and behaviours.
- Admit your mistakes and learn from them.
- Understand that accountability comes with consequences.
- Embrace the changes and improvements that accountabilty brings.
- Don't make it personal!

Things we must do and learn!

- We must change the way we view accountability across the board.
- Stop blaming everyone else when you get caught doing something you shouldn't.
- Stop taking everything personally.
- We must strive to understand that accountability brings law and order to everyone.
- We must be firm, fair, and consistent!

Teamwork

Another issue we have when it comes to being mindful of the gap is the lack of teamwork. Just like many of our topics I believe the issue is we are not intentional enough about teaching everyone in our organization or family their role in understanding teamwork. This can be done in several ways, but we must put in the effort to make sure everyone understands the meaning of and need for teamwork.

If I asked what teamwork means I would probably get a few different answers, and many would be close. If we break it down, what does it mean to be a team? A team is a group of people who compete in a sport, game, etc., against another group: a group of people who work together: a group of two or more animals used to pull a wagon, cart, etc.: a number of persons associated together in work or activity: as a group on one side (as in football or a debate).

Now that we know what a team is let's look at the importance of teamwork. If you are familiar with a team of animals that pull a wagon or cart, what happens when they are not on the same page and want to go different directions? Yep, nothing good happens and if it is allowed to go on for very long something is going to get broken. Does that sound familiar at all? It should because it is exactly what is happening to many of you in your family unit or organization. You have forgotten the importance of working together to achieve your desired outcome. Now look around we are headed nowhere good, simply because we stopped working together.

I believe it is important to understand that what goes into a successful, effective, and efficient team are: good leadership; clear communication; establishing roles; knowing your role; conflict resolution; and setting a good example.

Good Leadership: Effective leadership is one of the most important components of good teamwork. The team's leader should possess the skills to create and maintain a positive working environment and motivate and inspire the team members to take a positive approach to work and be highly committed. An effective team leader will promote a high level of morale and make their team feel supported and valued. Just remember morale is everyone's responsibility not just the leaders!

"Leadership is a matter of having people look at you and gain confidence, seeing how you

TEAMWORK

react. If you're in control, they're in control."
Tom Landry

Clear Communication: Communication is a vital factor of all interpersonal interaction and especially that of a team. Team members must be able to articulate their feelings, express plans, and goals, share ideas and see each other's viewpoints. Remember the need for communication and the challenges we addressed earlier.

Establishing Roles: It is absolutely necessary for team members to understand what their role on the team is, what he/she is responsible for. This also shows value for each team member and what happens if they do not carry their weight or perform to the established standard. The team leader can enable this by defining the purpose in a clear-cut manner in the beginning of the formation of the team. This is an absolute must if we are going to work together as a team and close or bridge the gap!

"Build for your team a feeling of oneness, of dependence on one another and of strength to be derived by unity." Vince Lombardi

Knowing Your Role: It's not enough for us to merely establish roles within an organization. We must make sure that each person knows their role and value within the organization. We must also teach them to understand the role and value of everyone else! This will in turn teach them the importance and understanding of each specific role and why it is needed. Not everyone can be the quarterback, someone has to block, carry the ball, etc. This is where we must be cautious because some people would rather let the quarterback get sacked than do their job! If we learn to work together, we all add more value to the overall team.

Conflict Resolution: Conflicts will arise no matter how well a team functions together. The best way to counter conflict is to have structured methods of conflict resolution. Team members should be able to voice their concerns without fear of offending others. Instead of avoiding conflict issues, a hands-on approach that resolves them quickly is much better. It is often advised that the team leader sits with the conflicting parties and helps work out their differences without taking sides and trying to remain objective if possible. This is an absolute must if we are going to be an efficient and effective team!

Set A Good Example: The team leader must set a good example for good teamwork to come about. In order to keep team members positive and committed and motivated, the team leader herself/himself needs to exhibit these qualities. The team looks to the leader for support and guidance so any negativity on the leader's part can be disastrous. We must get better at

TEAMWORK

setting a positive example for others to follow. This adds value across the board for the team, the individuals, and the organization!

Teamwork provides a way to work together and establish an identity. This is paramount in today's world of recruiting, retention, and succession planning. Especially for my brothers and sisters in law enforcement. We must establish our identity and it must be positive and valuable to attract and keep folks. It also adds value to how we deal with all of our stakeholders in good times and bad.

You must truly understand your role and what value it brings to the organization.

- Know your role.
- Know/understand others role.
- Understand your value.
- Work together.
- Understand each other.

No matter what your role is, you must set the example for others to follow.

- People emulate what they see.
- All supervisors are leaders.
- All employees are leaders.
- Set the tone for others to follow.
- Be positive no matter what is happening!

CLOSING THE GAP BY BUILDING BRIDGES FOR ORGANIZATIONAL AND PERSONAL SUCCESS!

Do you bring value to the team, or are you working against the other members? Organization?

- Are you accountable to others?
- Are you positive or negative?
- Are you a valued team member?
- Do you tarnish the team, organization, and self?

Understanding Teamwork and My Value

▶ When things are hard, don't make it personal!

▶ Accept responsiblity for your actions and behaviours.

▶ Know your role inside the organization.

▶ Value yourself and those around you.

▶ Set the example and stop worrying about everyone else.

▶ When things are not easy, don't make it personal!

Understanding Teamwork and My Value:

- **Surround yourself with people of Character!**
- Remain positive no matter what.
- **Find a mentor that will help you grow!**
- Self-reflect as needed.
- **Be a good teammate!**

Dealing with Difficult People

How often do we have to deal with difficult people? Probably much more than we want to. And for those in a service industry or customer service field way more than we should. No matter how good we are at customer service we are always going to deal with difficult people.

To better understand how to deal with difficult people we must try to understand what makes them difficult. One way is comparing them to ourselves when we are difficult to deal with. Here is the reality check: If we are honest all of us have been difficult to deal with in certain situations. The key is always how long do we allow the situation or person to make us difficult to deal with?

What makes people difficult to deal with on occasion or daily? Some people are just naturally difficult to understand; they may even be misunderstood. This could be due to their demeanor, tone, communications, communication style, etc. It could be a poor exchange of information; past or present. How often do we experience this when trying to resolve issues or just communicating over the phone in customer service or simple communications? This could also be the result of bad/poor communication, transmitted or conveyed. Remember how often it could come out wrong or misconstrued (70%)? What about the bad attitude that isn't our fault? Yeah, I'm kidding that is absolutely our responsibility and our choice. Therefore, that bad attitude is our fault.

Other things that can contribute to someone being an all-around difficult person may include past and present experiences, living or working in a toxic environment, or being around a constant negative influence. Perception of the organization, current problem (s) of the individual and the organization. Lack of planning, we are in a rush, so we expect everyone else to be in a rush. The urgency of the situation is important to me so it must be important to you. There could be any number of reasons someone has become a difficult person. Take a little time to self-reflect and determine what were the causes when you were that difficult person. Once you have completed that determine how you are going to strive daily to not be difficult.

If we are minding the gap and striving to build a bridge, we must learn how to deal with difficult people.

Naturally difficult to understand, the often-misunderstood person:

- Listen to them.
- Seek to understand what they are about.
- What is the issue/problem?

Poor exchange of information; past or present:

- What is the issue/problem?
- Be knowledgeable.
- Give correct information when asked.
- Improve communication by listening.

Bad attitude:

- Be kind and courteous.
- Problem solve, stay focused on the issue, not the attitude.
- Maintain a positive attitude.
- Show respect no matter what the issues are, or the attitude displayed.

Poor communication, transmitted or conveyed:

- Listen to issues and problem solve but listen first.
- Provide correct information.
- Strive for guidance/understanding about their need or issues.

- Admit if you or we messed up but don't blame anyone.

Past and present experiences:

- Admit if you or we messed up but don't blame anyone.
- Strive for guidance/understanding about their need or issues.
- Listen, listen, listen.
- Provide correct information.
- Be kind and courteous no matter what!

Toxic environment or influence:

- Be positive, no matter what.
- Be kind and courteous.
- Listen, listen, listen.
- Focus on the desired outcome. Problem solve, resolve the concern or issue.
- Change the perception of the environment or culture.

Perception of the organization:

- Admit if you or we messed up but don't blame anyone.
- Listen and understand.
- Change the perception for the positive!
- Focus on the desired outcome!

DEALING WITH DIFFICULT PEOPLE

Current problem (s):

- Listen to understand.
- Understand the problem and communicate.
- Problem solve, resolve the concern or issue.
- Provide as much guidance as you can.

If we can learn to better understand and deal with people, it will become much easier to deal with folks when they are difficult. The better I understand the more I will learn that I can sometimes be that difficult person that no one likes to deal with!

Things we must always do:

- Be professional, kind, and courteous.

CLOSING THE GAP BY BUILDING BRIDGES FOR ORGANIZATIONAL AND PERSONAL SUCCESS!

- Provide correct information.
- Listen to understand.
- Improve communication.
- Remain positive and helpful.
- Problem solve.
- Admit, but don't blame.
- Focus on the desired outcome.

As we take some time to self-reflect on how we are acting, we should look at how we are dealing with difficult people. Do we meet all the negativity and resistance with equal or greater force? Or are we striving to be better, so we do not become difficult people? Ask yourself how do I deal with people? Am I dealing with them positively or negatively? Do I remain calm and in control? Am I kind and courteous? Do I focus on the desired outcome? Am I a problem solver or creator? Am I providing good communication with correct information? Do I give guidance and understanding? Am I providing service with an attitude: good or bad? Some of these questions can be difficult to answer if we are struggling in any way, shape, form, or fashion in any area.

If we want to bridge the gap and learn how to deal with difficult people and not become one, we must take some time to learn how to be better. We must take some time to self-reflect. Take some time to understand the impact of our attitude. We must surround ourselves with Mentors who will help guide us.

We must learn to control our thoughts, speech, and actions. Be willing to make changes as needed in your thoughts, speech, and actions. Remain calm when dealing with difficult people. Strive to not become difficult to deal with ourselves!

Getting help:

- Self-reflect daily.
- Surround yourself with some good, trusted mentors.
- Remember if you make mistakes correct them and learn from them.
- Change your influence, friends, advisors, etc.
- Guard your thoughts, speech, and actions.
- Be accountable!

Things we must do and learn!

- Learn as much as you can about the challenges you face when dealing with difficult people.
- Keep the desired outcome in mind in all situations.
- Be accountable for your thoughts, speech, and actions.
- Get help: mentor (s), people of character.
- Know the mission of your organization and know your role.
- Remain calm and in control!

Connections

I have seen many leaders and even regular folks who were very good at working through the room. Some would even say they had charisma. All of us know someone like that that we say I wish I could connect like they do. They seem to come into a room and people will flock to them or want to meet them. Again, you know people that are like this. It might even be you. I can do this, it's just not my comfort zone. I constantly strive to get better at connecting with everyone I encounter. It's been part of my daily work life for nearly the last 29 years. If you are in the service industry you must learn to connect at least a little bit. However, I believe we have a huge gap when it comes to our overall connections. I believe that much of what we see sometimes is surface connections that feel great at first until you realize there is no foundation to the connection.

What we observed in that meeting, gala, or event was that person who had the appearance of connecting. Don't get mad yet. I'm not saying that many of those folks are not genuine when they make those connections. What I am merely pointing out is there remains a huge gap in connections built on a foundation of mutual respect, trust, and desire to build or grow a relationship or partnership. If I as a leader want to lead well, I must find a way to truly connect with my people and my stakeholders. Unfortunately, many use this as a tool of what can you do for me, if you have something I want I will attempt to connect. If you do not have anything I want or need I will surface connect because it looks good to the masses.

We must become better at connecting even if it is just a passing meeting or encounter. We must strive to be able to treat the janitor and executive each with the same level of commitment and respect to build a stronger relationship with our connections. I know there are many levels of relationships and partnerships. What I mean is that when we encounter folks, we have to approach it with genuine sincerity that we just want to be cordial and pleasant, and we are that way with everyone. If we encounter someone, we must build a relationship with or form a partnership with we don't have to make any adjustments because we approach every encounter as an opportunity to connect and possibly build a relationship.

If we want to close the gap, we must be mindful of our attitudes and actions when we surface-connect. We must understand that many folks see right through our efforts when we are not sincere and are merely playing a game. We will have folks that are just acquaintances, we must understand that is all they are, nothing more. We will have friendly folks, and maybe we work with them and talk to them often, this relationship is deeper than the acquaintance, but not yet a true friend. Leaders and employees struggle here because we often confuse these thinking they are deeper than they really are. We then have a relationship where it is a deep-rooted friendship or mentorship where someone genuinely cares for us and about us, these relationships are important for our growth and development. There is a partnership that has the same likes and dislikes, needs, and wants, common ground, and commitment to work, play, and or live together. The partnership means we are in everything together no matter what!

Connection: a relationship in which a person, thing, or idea is linked or associated with something else.

Relationships/Partnerships

As we take time to self-reflect let's look at our opportunities to build those relationships or partnerships. Most people have a desire to build relationships and many hope that they will experience a partnership that makes life easier. I know some of you are saying I don't even like people. Maybe not but life is easier and more fulfilling when we have some relationships and partnerships formed with respect, trust, communication, care, compassion, and love. Why do you think so many people struggle with connections? First, we don't put in the work and stay committed. Second, when relationships or partnerships get hard, we bail out or give up. Third, we misunderstand the purpose or significance of a good strong relationship or partnership that adds to our value and that of any family or organization. Fourth, we have the mindset that we do not need anyone.

For example, in the policing world, every encounter is a chance to connect. How we view it and interact with others will play a huge role in whether we create a relationship or not. It's the same when talking about customer service. You only get one opportunity to make a good first impression. Sometimes you don't get an opportunity to change that first impression. So, it is paramount we do our best to not come across as a surface connector in our encounters. Remember in both of these worlds we are there to serve others. The better we connect and understand each other the better we can serve each other. Which is what it is about at the end of the day! As police officers, firemen, or first responders, why would we not be out there building relationships and creating partnerships with everyone? I always teach any of those in my classes or who work with me this concept: I never want the first encounter with anyone that we serve on their worst possible day to be the first time we have attempted to connect. If we have been out there connecting, and building relationships then we are going to create partnerships. It makes it much easier when we have to deal with situations or incidents if we have connected. We must make sure that we have the mindset not just to protect and serve, but to connect and serve!

Relationship: how two or more concepts, objects, or people are connected, the state of being connected. How two or more people or groups regard and behave toward each other.

Partnership: the state of being a partner or partners, an association of two or more people working together.

Community

When I bring up community, I want to make sure everyone understands it's not just the law enforcement field, it's all of them. This could be your chosen work field, church, city where you work, or where you live. This could be your family, your friends, or any group or organization you affiliate with over time.

What does community even mean? A group of people living in the same place or having a particular characteristic in common. A feeling of fellowship with others, as a result of common attitudes, interests, and goals. So, process those definitions for a bit. Did you discover anything that might be the reason you either thrive or struggle in community building? As I reflect on the meaning, I can't help but go back to the beginning of connections. If I can't find a way to bridge the gap there is no way I'm building a relationship with anyone, let alone a partnership.

There is no way we can mind the gap if we do not spend some time understanding what it means to form connections. The purpose is so we can get better at connecting in order to build stronger relationships and create formidable partnerships. We are better together but we must strive to better understand each other to build respect, trust, and relationships. We must learn the true meaning of each of these as we go about our daily routines. We must understand the need to be part of a community, whatever that looks like for you. But, if we choose and we are free to choose to be part of something we must understand it only works if we do it together, and we are on the same page.

Things we must do and learn!

- Learn and understand what connections mean, and why they are important.

CLOSING THE GAP BY BUILDING BRIDGES FOR ORGANIZATIONAL AND PERSONAL SUCCESS!

- Learn and understand relationships and partnerships.
- Understand why all of these are needed to build community.
- Self-reflect on your relationships, partnerships, and community.
- What are you bringing to the table? Surface connection? Relationship building? Creating partnerships?
- How is your community?
- Are you part of something good or bad?
- What is your contribution in this area, at work, at home, or in your community?
- We must find at least one mentor and surround ourselves with trusted advisors.
- We must learn to grow and develop together to close the gap in our connections.

Consistency

Why does it seem like consistency is hard? We often know exactly what needs to be done and much of the time how to do it. Yet for some reason in this chaotic world of ours, we forget one of the most important things in life, consistency. If we took some time to break down the issues and why there constantly seems to be a gap in everything we do. I'm pretty confident we would find the lack of consistency as a constant in our lives. One of the biggest things we can count on is the lack of consistency.

So, how do we turn this around? Why is it so important that we figure out how to be more consistent in our daily lives? First, we must recognize the need for consistency in everything we do. Think about this: if we are inconsistent in our attitude, behavior, demeanor, communication, teamwork, leadership, accountability, or mindset, then how do we close the gap? How do we even bridge the gap if we are not consistent in these things?

What I have learned over the years is that this is an area where many leaders have issues. The problem is many do not want to admit this and do not want to put in the effort to make it better. Think about a time when a change had to be implemented or was expected. How did you as an individual and as an agency handle the change? Was there an effort by any leader to make sure that everyone was on the same page? Did anyone say here is how we accept and embrace these changes, because this is how we want to approach all change in the future? All I'm suggesting is that in something as simple as an expected change we can bring consistency. However, the reality is we usually do not handle them the same way, we are usually all over the place.

Over the course of my adult life, I have learned that consistency is a foundation from which I can build. I have had the privilege of working for several different agencies and each one has been unique in their needs and function. What I have observed is people need consistency. They need to know that the leader is going to be there. Simply showing up every day is showing commitment and consistency. They need to know the leader is going to make decisions and those will be based on the desired outcome. Folks need to know there is a desired outcome and that everyone will work together to get there. You can't be on board one day and against everything the next day. Folks need to know that the leader and the supervisor have their back. It's kind of crazy but just being available is a form of consistency. When we fail to grasp the gravity of the situation and the needs of the people, we only add to the gap we don't close, nor do we bridge it. If we want to build relationships/partnerships we must be consistent, we must find ways to connect with everyone as soon as possible.

Unfortunately, we get lazy or tired or maybe even a bit disenchanted with life, work, and/or people. This causes us to become distracted and we lose focus on everything. How can I be consistent in anything if I'm dealing with all these emotions? Throw in some frustration, anger, or chaos and I start to become sporadic in everything that I do. Man, when we deal with people and emotions things can become complicated and distracting. The problem is most of us deal with people all day, every day. This is why it is so important to remain focused on our why and be consistent in our thoughts, speech, and actions. All of these must set the example for positive growth and progression in our personal and professional lives. If we know there is a gap, how do we close it and then build a bridge to move forward?

My hope is that you take some time throughout your reading of this book and really look at the gap (s) in your life. Look at them as individuals in your personal life and look at them as a person and organization in your professional life. Think about some of the root causes of the gaps you have identified. Many of us will have the same issues, but many will be unique to our own situations. In order to learn and grow we must identify the underlying issues and then develop a game plan to solve the problem. How do we solve problems? We must be intentional and disciplined! If we break it down isn't inconsistency merely the lack of intent and discipline?

What does it even mean to be consistent? The actual definition is acting or done the same way over time, especially to be fair or accurate, unchanging in nature, standard, or agreement. In other words, it means to be dependable, logical, reliable, steady, or true for your own thoughts, speech, and actions. If we set a standard or guideline we must adhere to the standard or guideline the same way over time. If not, then why is it the standard or guideline in the first place? One of the worst things someone can do is be inconsistent in their daily interactions and interpretations of policy, procedure, and standard guidelines.

Remember we talked about the fact that almost everyone has some form of policy, procedure, standard or guideline? We establish these to provide a guideline of how we are supposed to function daily. These are designed to protect both the individual and the organization, and when followed consistently do a pretty good job of it. What we must realize is that if we begin

CONSISTENCY

to deviate from our written standards or guidelines, we are damaging our foundation and creating a bigger gap! We have enough on our plate with the built-in gaps of age, experience, shift work, organization structure, and differing mindsets, that we should not be creating more by being inconsistent. If we deviate here our communication suffers, our accountability is all over the place, and our ability to establish a positive environment and culture is non-existent. All due to our lack of intent and discipline to do things the way we should consistently for everyone no matter the person or situation.

Most of you are familiar with the processes we use sometimes when conducting promotional or hiring boards, and interviews. There is usually a scenario question or two where we ask something about integrity or honesty. We are trying to establish the importance of learning what is accepted behavior and what is not accepted based on our own already-established set of rules or guidelines. We are basically looking for what you say you will do and if it matches what you actually do in every situation. If you see something inappropriate you will act and/or report if it is the proper way to handle the person and the situation. There are a number I have used and been asked myself; most have to do with an inappropriate action or behavior by someone near you. This could be a co-worker, supervisor, or even a stranger. What the board or panel wants to see is you doing the right thing and speaking up and/or reporting the incident or situation to the appropriate person or persons. You will not condone inappropriate behavior or actions because it is not consistent with the already established policy, procedure, or standard. If the candidate answers anyway other than acting to stop and report the person and situation they are usually not moved forward in the promotional or hiring process. In most places that is an automatic disqualification.

Let's fast forward to the candidate who answered the question the right way based on the established standard. They are now hired and striving to become valued, productive members of your organization. They are going about their own business one day when they observe some inappropriate behavior by a co-worker or supervisor, and they take action and speak up and report it immediately. In many places out there what happens next? Is the person and situation addressed or do we now label the person who saw something, said something and intervened as the issue? Unfortunately, the answer is we label them and they nor anyone else in our organization will ever speak up against negativity, inappropriate behavior, or any other issue that arises. Our inconsistency just made the negative, inappropriate behavior an accepted practice. We also just created an environment and culture that will continue to enable bad behavior and

CONSISTENCY

attitudes. "If the standard was the standard to get hired, it must remain the standard to remain part of the organization!" We must be consistent in everything we think, say, or do!

If we are minding the gap, then we must be intentional and disciplined to establish and maintain a level of consistency that can withstand anything that gets thrown at it. At some point, we must get out of our own way and bridge this gap. We must take a long hard look at the things we are allowing and the things we need to improve to be consistent with our own established policy, procedure, or standard. We must stop lowering the standard and require folks to rise to our standard if we ever really want to close and/or bridge the gap.

Things we must learn and do:

- Learn what consistency means as an individual and an organization.
- Understand the need for self-reflection.
- We must be intentional to meet and even exceed the standard.
- We must be disciplined to maintain our consistency no matter who or what we are facing.
- We must understand how everything connects to our consistency: communication, accountability, attitude, behavior, and mindset.

CLOSING THE GAP BY BUILDING BRIDGES FOR ORGANIZATIONAL AND PERSONAL SUCCESS!

- We must be aware of the gap and our contribution to close/bridge it or make it wider!
- We must be on guard daily for what we think, say, or do.
- Everyone must be aware of their level of influence and the folks that are watching us daily!

Don't ever take lightly the responsibility we all have in creating a positive, healthy, growing, and developing mindset and culture in our personal and professional lives. This can be accomplished by being intentional, disciplined, and consistent.

Spiritual

This one may open a can of worms, but I feel prompted to include it anyway. Please understand my intent with anything I write or talk about is not to make someone mad. I merely want us to start thinking about how we are contributing to the increasing of the gap or closing/bridging the gap. The reality is there is a huge gap in how we look at things spiritually. Much of this is due to our own upbringing and established beliefs. Our character that we have built and the morals we have established. Remember they are merely how we carry ourselves and what we find is acceptable and what we find unacceptable. Understanding this and learning the root cause of our behaviors and actions has been an ongoing debate for thousands of years. Not here to judge but some of you out there are completely clueless! Again, do not forget I may tell you something you need to hear, maybe not something you want to hear.

I'm not here to regurgitate the Bible or any lesson included there within. But man does it provide a really great guideline of how we are supposed to do things! An established set of guidelines that would help all of us in our daily interactions and reactions if we just read, understood, and applied the information. Look, we are all different in many ways, but all created the same way (consistency). We have all been given information and allowed to understand and even translate it for our own meaning to match our own unique beliefs and standards. The problem is we have done so in such a way that we constantly create a gap instead of building a bridge.

Take all the religion and your unique beliefs or interpretations out of it and just reflect for a moment or two. This spiritual aspect can be summed up like this. A standard or guideline was provided for us with the Bible. Some we like, and some are hard to follow. Just because they are hard doesn't mean we shouldn't follow them; just means they are hard. Lots of things that are best for us involve sacrifice, so even though they are hard we must strive to follow them as best we can. This doesn't mean we will be perfect; we won't be, we will fail. We fail because we are supposed to fail. These guidelines are established for the purpose of us to rely on a greater power (God) because we are not strong enough on our own. It's similar to relying on a leader or mentor to help you be the best you possible.

If we merely understand that our differences are what make us better, then we can begin to close and bridge the gap. We need all of our unique beliefs in order to make things work. If you have read the Bible, you know that there were many different ethnicities and folks that had very differing beliefs. The Bible was established so we could get a glimpse at the struggle that they all went through so many years ago. It was written to provide a guideline so that we would not struggle with the same issues they did. Well, that's the purpose but remember we are hardheaded and free to choose for ourselves. That is exactly what it is, a choice for us to follow or go against the recommendations provided, Sound familiar, just like our organizational guidelines!

Just like everything else we can't get on the same page when dealing with our spirituality. How many different religions do we have out there? How many times has a new church or religion been created because someone didn't like the interpretation of the WORD? Therein lies much of our problem when we don't like something or agree with something we change to fit instead of changing our behavior or practices to fit the established guidelines. Like it or not this is another reason we have such a gap in everything we encounter and do today. It all goes back to respect and understanding. We must respect each other and strive to understand each other. That does not mean we have to believe the same way or adhere to the same set of standards. It does mean that we must strive to work together and understand the need to follow a set of established rules and guidelines in order to learn and grow together. The Bible is a clear-cut set of standards and guidelines, just like our laws and rules established nationally and by state. Our Constitution is another set of rules or guidelines meant to be understood and followed. Neither of these was established with the belief that everyone would agree with every standard or guideline created. They were established to give us a working set of rules and guidelines to make us better. The Bible, U.S. Constitution, laws, and rules, were all created to remind us that we all must follow guidelines and we must work together to make them work.

How do we close the spiritual gap?

- We must understand the need for standards and guidelines (Bible).
- We must realize not everyone will follow the guidelines.
- Everyone must strive not to be judgmental.
- I can follow the rules and guidelines and not accept things that go against my beliefs.
- We can agree to disagree and still work alongside each other.
- We must work together to make a positive difference.

If we want to close the gap, we must follow our prompting in the Chronicles!

SPIRITUAL

If my people, who are called by name, will humble themselves and pray and seek my face and turn from their wicked ways, then I will hear from heaven, and I will forgive their sin and heal their land. 2 Chronicles 7:14

Conclusion

Hopefully, by now you have begun to spend some time doing some self-reflection. My goal throughout this book was and is to get each of you to understand the type of contribution you are making in creating or closing the gap. My prayer is that I have not offended you or made you mad in the process. However, if you got offended or mad, I would ask you to take some time to understand why. Am I the issue or was it anything I said or brought up? If this is you, then this book is definitely for you!

We spent time looking at everything from our ego, foundation, character, generational, communication, leadership, mental health, mindset, attitude, accountability, teamwork, dealing with difficult people, consistency, and finally spirituality. Understanding the impact that each of these has on whether we are creating the gap or building the bridge is paramount to our ability to work together and move forward positively. We must understand each one to completely grasp the need to be mindful of the gap and the ever-growing need to close or bridge the gap!

CONCLUSION

My prayer is that you have read and learned something along the way that will greatly influence you to strive to be part of the team that wants to close the gap and build a bridge for the space that cannot be closed. The challenge as we move forward is to become part of the solution and not continue to be part of the problem. However, we must work together for the desired outcome! Even if that is simply respect for each other and the unique differences we all bring to the table!

Things we must do and learn!

- We must be aware that the gap exists.
- We must be aware of our contribution to creating the gap.
- We must understand the need to close the gap and build a bridge!
- Everyone must work together to accomplish the desired outcome.
- We must be intentional and disciplined.
- Even when it is hard, we must keep striving to close the gap!
- Don't take or make anything personal!
- We will get out of this the same effort we put into it. If we do nothing or build nothing the gap remains the same or continues to grow.
- Self-reflect as needed.

- Surround yourself with trusted advisors to hold you accountable.
- Find at least one Mentor to teach, coach, and guide you to do things honorably.
- Ask for help when needed. Do not try this on your own.
- Be positive and set a good example for others to follow.
- We must answer the why for ourselves and others!
- Never give up, keep moving forward!

Let's partner together to close the gap and build the bridge so that we can learn, grow, and develop together. Strive every day to be mindful of the gap and our own contribution to creating it or building the bridge to cross it. Let's be positive and work together to make things better for our children and their children!

My challenge to you is let's work together to do something now not later to understand the gap, close what we can, and bridge what we can't close!

Mind the Gap! If we don't it will get bigger and bigger! Let's work together to close it and bridge what we can't close!

Dear Reader,

I would like to invite you to reach out to me at earl@earlmorrison.com if you need any encouragement or guidance. Check out my business website at https://earlmorrison.com for more information on Professional Leadership Development Training and Mentoring I offer.

I encourage you to connect with me on LinkedIn:

Earl Morrison, MSCJ, LCC: https://www.linkedin.com/in/earl-morrison-mscj-lcc-751022b3/

Find me on Facebook: Earl Morrison Leading and Learning with Character: https://www.facebook.com/EarlMorrisonLeadingandLearningwithCharacter

If you haven't already I would recommend you read my other books:

- Leadership Lessons Learned: Leading and Learning with Character
- Mentoring for Life!
- Jumpstart Your Leadership and Spiritual Growth: 119 Daily Devotions to Grow Your Leadership and Spiritual Walk with God

Have I not commanded you? Be strong and courageous. Do not be afraid; do not be discouraged, for the Lord your God will be with you wherever you go." Joshua 1:9
~Earl